INTRODUCTION

Butterflies and moths belong to the second largest order of insects (next to beetles) with approximately 170,000 species worldwide. All have two pairs of wings covered with overlapping layers of fine scales. They feed by uncoiling a long feeding tube (proboscis) and sucking nutrients from flowers, puddles, etc. When not in use, the tube is coiled under the head.

The two groups differ in several ways:

BUTTERFLIES
- Active by day
- Brightly colored
- Thin body
- Rests with wings held erect over its back
- Antennae are thin and thickened at the tip

MOTHS
- Active at night
- Most are dull-colored
- Stout body
- Rests with wings folded, tent-like, over its back
- Antennae are usually thicker and often feathery

All butterflies and moths have a complex life cycle consisting of four developmental stages.

1. **EGGS** – Eggs are laid singly or in clusters on vegetation or on the ground. One or more clutches of eggs may be laid each year.
2. **CATERPILLARS (LARVAE)** – These worm-like creatures hatch from eggs and feed primarily on plants (often on the host plant on which the eggs were laid). As they grow, larvae shed their skin periodically.
3. **PUPAE** – Pupae are the "cases" within which caterpillars transform into adults. The pupa of a butterfly is known as a chrysalis; those of moths are called cocoons. In cooler regions, pupae often overwinter before maturing into butterflies or moths.
4. **ADULT** – Butterflies/moths emerge from pupae to feed and breed.

ATTRACTING BUTTERFLIES TO YOUR YARD

1. **Food** – Almost all butterfly caterpillars eat plants; adult butterflies feed almost exclusively on plant nectar. Your local garden shop, library and bookstore will have information on which plants attract specific species.
2. **Water** – Soak the soil in your garden or sandy areas to create puddles. These provide a source of water and minerals.
3. **Rocks** – Put large flat rocks in sunny areas. Butterflies will gather there to spread their wings and warm up.
4. **Brush** – Small brush piles and hollow logs provide ideal places for butterflies to lay their eggs and hibernate over the winter.

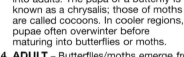

Most illustrations show the upper wings of males unless otherwise noted. The measurements denote the wingspan of species. Note that wing shape differs in flight and at rest. Illustrations are not to scale.

Waterford Press produces reference guides that introduce novices to nature, science, outdoor recreation and survival. Product information is featured on the website: www.waterfordpress.com

Text and illustrations © 2020 by Waterford Press Inc. All rights reserved. Cover image © Shutterstock.
To order, call 800-434-2555.
For permissions, or to share comments, e-mail editor@waterfordpress.com. For information on custom-published products, call 800-434-2555 or e-mail info@waterfordpress.com.

ISBN 978-1-62005-451-2
$7.95 U.S.
Made in the USA

MINNESOTA BUTTERFLIES & POLLINATORS

MINNESOTA BUTTERFLIES & POLLINATORS

Kavanagh/Leung

A Folding Pocket Guide to Familiar Species

SWALLOWTAILS & ALLIES

This family includes the largest butterfly species. Most are colorful and have a tail-like projection on each hindwing.

Zebra Swallowtail
Eurytides marcellus To 3.5 in. (9 cm)
Note white-tipped "tails" and red spot near base of hindwings.

Giant Swallowtail
Papilio cresphontes
To 6 in. (15 cm)
One of the largest North American butterflies.

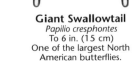

Black Swallowtail
Papilio polyxenes To 3.5 in. (9 cm)
Note two rows of yellow spots on forewings and orange spots on hindwings.

Canadian Tiger Swallowtail
Papilio canadensis
To 3 in. (8 cm)
A smaller version of the Eastern Tiger Swallowtail.

Spicebush Swallowtail
Papilio troilus
To 4.5 in. (11 cm)
Note greenish hindwings.

Eastern Tiger Swallowtail
Papilio glaucus To 6 in. (15 cm)

WHITES & SULPHURS

White and yellow/orange butterflies are among the first to appear in spring.

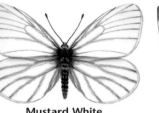

Mustard White
Artogeia oleracea To 2 in. (5 cm)
Common in moist forests. Feeds on a variety of mustards.

Cabbage White
Pieris rapae To 2 in. (5 cm)
One of the most common butterflies. Feeds on cabbage leaves and wild mustards.

WHITES & SULPHURS

Olympia Marblewing
Euchloe olympia
To 1.5 in. (4 cm)
Common in open areas and along lakeshores.

Orange Sulphur
Colias eurytheme
To 2.5 in. (6 cm)
Gold-orange butterfly has a prominent forewing spot.

Pink-edged Sulphur
Colias interior
To 1.75 in. (4.2 cm)

Common Sulphur
Colias philodice To 2 in. (5 cm)
Common in open areas and along roadsides.

Southern Dogface
Zerene cesonia
To 2.5 in. (6 cm)
Note poodle-head pattern on forewings.

Dainty Sulphur
Nathalis iole
To 1.25 in. (3.2 cm)

GOSSAMER-WINGED BUTTERFLIES

This family of small bluish or coppery butterflies often has small, hair-like tails on its hindwings. Most rest with their wings folded and underwings exposed.

Spring Azure
Celastrina ladon To 1.25 in. (3.2 cm)
One of the earliest spring butterflies.

Saepiolus Blue
Plebejus saepiolus To 1.25 in. (3.2 cm)
Feeds primarily on clovers.

GOSSAMER-WINGED BUTTERFLIES

Upperwings   Underwings

Coral Hairstreak
Harkenclenus titus
To 1.5 in. (4 cm)
Note reddish spots along margin of hindwings. Upperwings are brownish.

Orange Sulphur *(Eastern Tailed Blue)*
Eastern Tailed Blue
Cupido comyntas
To 1 in. (3 cm)
Note orange spots above thread-like hindwing tails.

Purplish Copper
Lycaena helloides
To 1.25 in. (3.2 cm)
Purplish sheen is most evident in bright sunlight.

American Copper
Lycaena phlaeas
To 1.25 in. (3.2 cm)
Common in disturbed areas and along roadsides.

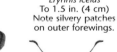

Harvester
Feniseca tarquinius
To 1.25 in. (3.2 cm)
North America's only carnivorous butterfly feeds primarily on aphids.

Brown Elfin
Incisalia augustinus
To 1 in. (3 cm)
Underwings are chocolate-brown.

Bronze Copper
Hyllolycaena hyllus
To 2 in. (5 cm)
Common in wet meadows and near waterways.

GOSSAMER-WINGED BUTTERFLIES

Upperwings   Underwings

Acadian Hairstreak
Satyrium acadica
To 1.5 in. (4 cm)
Grayish hairstreak is common in wet areas.

SKIPPERS

Named for their fast, bouncing flight, skippers have distinctive antennae that end in curved clubs.

Arctic Skipper
Carterocephalus palaemon
To 1 in. (3 cm)

Dreamy Duskywing
Erynnis icelus
To 1.5 in. (4 cm)
Note silvery patches on outer forewings.

Common Sootywing
Pholisora catullus
To 1.25 in. (3.2 cm)
Forewings have two curved rows of white spots. Found in open and disturbed areas.

Northern Cloudywing
Thorybes pylades
To 1.75 in. (4.5 cm)
Common in open areas near flowers and mud puddles.

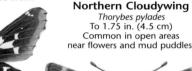

Underwings

Silver-spotted Skipper
Epargyreus clarus
To 2.5 in. (6 cm)
Has a large, irregular silver patch on the underside of its hindwings. Patch is absent on the forewings.

Common Branded Skipper
Hesperia comma
To 1.25 in. (3.2 cm)

BRUSHFOOTS

This family is named for its small forelegs that they use to "taste" food.

Milbert's Tortoiseshell
Aglais milberti To 2 in. (5 cm)

Viceroy
Limenitis archippus
To 3 in. (8 cm)
Told from similar Monarch by its smaller size and the thin, black band on its hindwings.

White Admiral
Limenitis arthemis
To 3 in. (8 cm)
Common in upland deciduous forests.

Large Wood Nymph
Cercyonis pegala
To 3 in. (8 cm)
Note 2 "eyespots" on the forewing. Yellow band is not always present.

Silvery Checkerspot
Chlosyne nycteis
To 2 in. (5 cm)

Meadow Fritillary
Boloria bellona
To 2 in. (5 cm)
Found in meadows and along streams and hillsides.

Northern Pearly-eye
Enodia anthedon
To 2 in. (5 cm)
Common in clearings and deciduous woodlands.

Common Ringlet
Coenonympha tullia
To 1.5 in. (4 cm)
Flies close to the ground. Found in grassy areas.

BRUSHFOOTS

Upperwings

Monarch
Danaus plexippus
To 4 in. (10 cm)
Note rows of white spots on edges of wings. Millions migrate between the US and the forests of central Mexico each year.
Minnesota's state insect.

Underwings

Mourning Cloak
Nymphalis antiopa
To 3.5 in. (9 cm)
Emerges during the first spring thaw. Found in a variety of habitats.

Little Wood Satyr
Megisto cymela
To 2 in. (5 cm)
Note 2 "eyespots" on each wing.

Compton Tortoiseshell
Nymphalis vaualbum
To 3 in. (8 cm)
Note ragged wings.

Pearly Crescentspot
Phyciodes tharos
To 1.5 in. (4 cm)
Note black margins on wings. Hindwing is marked with dark crescent-shaped spots.

Question Mark
Polygonia interrogationis
To 2.5 in. (6 cm)
Note lilac margin on wings. Underwings feature a silvery patch that resembles a question mark on the first spring thaw.

Upperwings

Gray Comma
Polygonia progne
To 2 in. (5 cm)
Underwings are grayish and feature a silvery comma mark on the hindwing.

Underwings

BRUSHFOOTS

Eyed Brown
Satyrodes eurydice
To 2 in. (5 cm)
Note 4 spots on forewings and 6 spots on hindwings.

Great Spangled Fritillary
Speyeria cybele
To 3 in. (8 cm)
Common in marshes and wet meadows.

Red Admiral
Vanessa atalanta
To 2.5 in. (6 cm)
Dark butterfly has prominent orange bars on forewings and border of hindwings.

Baltimore Checkerspot
Euphydryas phaeton
To 2.5 in. (6 cm)

American Lady
Vanessa virginiensis
To 2 in. (5 cm)
Underside of hindwings feature prominent "eyespots."

Buckeye
Junonia coenia
To 2.5 in. (6 cm)
Note orange wing bars on forewings and 8 distinct "eyespots."

Painted Lady
Vanessa cardui
To 2.5 in. (6 cm)
Tip of forewing is dark with white spots. Underwings have four iridescent blue-black spots on the hindwing.

Upperwings

Underwings

MOTHS

Eastern Tent Caterpillar Moth
Malacosoma americanum
To 1.5 in. (4 cm)
Communal web nests are a common sight on trees and shrubs, especially fruit trees.

Hummingbird Clearwing
Hemaris thysbe
To 2 in. (5 cm)
Wings have clear patches. Hovers near flowers like a hummingbird.

Cecropia Moth
Hyalophora cecropia
To 6 in. (15 cm)
Note white, crescent-shaped marks on hindwings.

Columbia Silk Moth
Hyalophora columbia
To 4 in. (10 cm)

Polyphemus Moth
Antheraea polyphemus
To 6 in. (15 cm)

Fall Webworm Moth
Hyphantria cunea
To 1.5 in. (4 cm)
Larvae live in a communal web and attack over 100 species of trees.

Five-spotted Hawk Moth
Manduca quinquemaculata
To 5.5 in. (14 cm)
Caterpillars feed on tomato, potato and tobacco plants. Caterpillar (also known as Tomato Hornworm) has a green horn at its rear.

Cabbage Looper
Trichoplusia ni
To 1.5 in. (4 cm)
Named for the behavior of the caterpillar, which "inches" forward with an arched back as it moves.

OTHER POLLINATORS

About 75% of the crop plants grown worldwide depend on pollinators – bees, butterflies, birds, bats and other animals – for fertilization and reproduction. Although some species of plants are pollinated by the wind and water, the vast majority (almost 90%) need the help of animals to act as pollinating agents. More than 1,000 of the world's most important foods, beverages and medicines are derived from plants that require pollination by animals.

Pollinating animals worldwide are threatened due to loss of habitat, introduced and invasive species, pesticides, diseases and parasites.

Bees, Wasps & Flies

North America is home to approximately 4,000 species of bees. Of these, the most important crop pollinators are wild native honey bees and managed colonies of European honey bees. Other important flying insects include bumble bees, mason bees, carpenter bees, wasps and numerous flies. With honey bee populations in a huge decline due to certain illnesses and habitat loss, this can have a huge impact on food production in North America.

HONEY BEE ANATOMY

Beetles

The living jewels of the bug world, beetles are the dominant life group on the earth with about 400,000 species found in all habitats except the polar regions and the oceans. They are invaluable to ecosystems as both pollinators and scavengers, feeding on dead animals and fallen trees to recycle nutrients back into the soil. Some, however, are serious pests and cause great harm to living plants (trees, crops). Learn to recognize the good from the bad and involve your local land management and pest control resources to mitigate the spread of harmful beetles.

BEETLE ANATOMY

Birds, Bats & Other Animals

More than 50 species of North American birds occasionally feed on plant nectar and blossoms, but it is the primary food source for hummingbirds and orioles. Sugar water feeders are a good way to supplement the energy of nectar drinkers, but it is far better to plant flowers and shrubs that provide native sources of nutrient-rich nectar. While very common in tropical climates around the world, only three species of nectar-feeding bats are found in the southwestern U.S. They are important pollinators of desert plants including large cacti (organ pipe, saguaro), agaves and century plants. Rodents, lizards and small mammals like mice also pollinate plants when feeding on their nectar and flower heads.

Ruby-throated Hummingbird

Long-nosed Bat

OTHER POLLINATORS

Attracting Bees & Other Pollinators

- Recognize the pollinators in your area and plant gardens to support the larvae and adults of different species.
- Cultivate native pollen and nectar-producing plants that bloom at different times throughout the growing season. Ensure the species you select will thrive with the amount of sunshine and moisture at the site. Reduce/eliminate use of pesticides. If you use any type of repellent, ensure it is organic and pesticide-free.
- The plants that attract birds, butterflies and moths for pollination most commonly have bright red, orange or yellow flowers with very little scent. Butterflies prefer flat-topped "cluster" flowers. Hummingbirds prefer tube or funnel-shaped flowers.
- Create areas, out of the sun, where pollinators can rest and avoid predation while foraging.
- Supply water for both drinking and bathing. Create shallow puddles for bees and butterflies.
- Create nesting boxes or brushy areas that provide protection from predation and are suitable for pollinators to raise their young.
- Learn to recognize the good and bad garden bugs.

CATERPILLARS

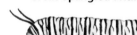

Tiger Swallowtail

Giant Swallowtail

Mourning Cloak

Great Spangled Fritillary

Sulphur

Monarch

Buckeye

Painted Lady

Five-spotted Hawk Moth
Note green horn at rear.

Cabbage Looper

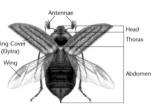

Fall Webworm Moth

Tent Caterpillar Moth

Webworm Web

Tent Caterpillar Web